Facts About the Weasel

By Lisa Strattin

© 2019 Lisa Strattin

FREE BOOK

FREE FOR ALL SUBSCRIBERS

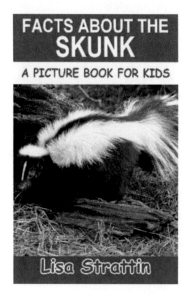

LisaStrattin.com/Subscribe-Here

BOX SET

- **FACTS ABOUT THE POISON DART FROGS**
- **FACTS ABOUT THE THREE TOED SLOTH**
  - **FACTS ABOUT THE RED PANDA**
  - **FACTS ABOUT THE SEAHORSE**
  - **FACTS ABOUT THE PLATYPUS**
  - **FACTS ABOUT THE REINDEER**
  - **FACTS ABOUT THE PANTHER**
- **FACTS ABOUT THE SIBERIAN HUSKY**

LisaStrattin.com/BookBundle

Facts for Kids Picture Books by Lisa Strattin

Little Blue Penguin, Vol 92

Chipmunk, Vol 5

Frilled Lizard, Vol 39

Blue and Gold Macaw, Vol 13

Poison Dart Frogs, Vol 50

Blue Tarantula, Vol 115

African Elephants, Vol 8

Amur Leopard, Vol 89

Sabre Tooth Tiger, Vol 167

Baboon, Vol 174

Sign Up for New Release Emails Here

LisaStrattin.com/subscribe-here

COVER IMAGE

https://flickr.com/photos/100915417@N07/50379873356/

ADDIITONAL IMAGES

https://flickr.com/photos/mikeprince/43847071394/

https://flickr.com/photos/firstmac/30795929410/

https://flickr.com/photos/mikeprince/43847063704/

https://flickr.com/photos/100915417@N07/50606359426/

https://flickr.com/photos/tom_twinhelix/3611525499/

https://flickr.com/photos/15016964@N02/6605882785/

https://flickr.com/photos/birdman_of_beaverton/46446449994/

https://flickr.com/photos/conifer/8393516695/

https://flickr.com/photos/conifer/8401089105/

https://flickr.com/photos/beckymatsubara/29906444027/

Contents

INTRODUCTION.. 9

CHARACTERISTICS 11

APPEARANCE 13

LIFE STAGES 15

LIFE SPAN 17

SIZE... 19

HABITAT... 21

DIET... 23

ENEMIES... 25

SUITABILITY AS PETS... 27

INTRODUCTION

The Weasel is a small meat-eating mammal that is found on every continent with the exception of Australia, the surrounding islands, as well as the cold polar regions. There are many weasel species that vary in size, color and behavior depending on where they live in the world.

The Common Weasel, also known as the European Weasel and the Least Weasel, is the most numerous and can be found across much of the northern hemisphere. These tiny but vicious predators are the smallest carnivorous mammals in the world.. Although Weasels are fairly common throughout much of their natural range, populations in certain areas have been affected by habitat loss and they are often seen as pests by farmers.

The ferocious and greedy nature of the Weasel has led to them getting a bad reputation especially with farmers who trap and kill them to prevent loss of livestock. They have however, been introduced to countries where they are not native because they are versatile and dominant in controlling other pests.

CHARACTERISTICS

The Weasel is a solitary animal that spends much of its life hunting for small prey on the ground during both the day and night. They are territorial animals that patrol their home ranges vigorously. Males and females tend to avoid each other except when mating.

Within their territory, they are known to make nests in crevices, tree roots and abandoned burrows where the weasel is able to rest safely. Weasels are strong and powerful, considering their small size, and are able to catch and kill animals that are much larger than they are, before carrying it back to their burrow.

In order to make sure that they have the best view of their surroundings, weasels are known to sit up on their hind legs exposing their white underside.

APPEARANCE

The weasel's long, slender bodies are perfectly suited for following mice into their burrows. They have a small, narrow head which is not much thicker than their neck. This feature, along with their short legs and flexible spine means that they are able to easily maneuver in small, confined spaces. They have a sharply pointed snout and triangular head, with small, rounded ears and black eyes. Their coat is dark or light brown on their head, back, legs and tail, with white on their underside. In areas further north, individuals will often change from brown to white in color so that they are camouflaged in the snow.

The weasel has pointed canine teeth which they use for biting and shearing the flesh of their prey. Their teeth are incredibly sharp and are capable of delivering a fatal bite to animals more than twice their size! They have five toes on each of their paws, tipped with small, non-retractable claws. Although these claws are mostly used for holding onto prey, their claws also help them burrow into the ground quickly.

LIFE STAGES

The only time weasels will tolerate one another is when a male and female meet to mate. After a gestation period that lasts for around five weeks, the female gives birth to a litter of between one and seven kittens in her burrow. Young weasels develop fast and are not only weaned by the time they are two months old but are also able to hunt small prey. They will leave their mother within the next few weeks to establish their own territory. Although females tend to live for around three years, they are not able to successfully breed until their second and third years. Males, however, tend to roam before they are a year old and are more vulnerable to numerous predators.

LIFE SPAN

Males generally live only about a year because they roam off by themselves at a young age and are taken by predators. Females usually live for 2-3 years.

SIZE

Weasels normally grow to be 9 to 15 inches long and weigh less than half a pound.

HABITAT

Weasels are found native to different habitats such as woodlands, coniferous forest and on grassy plains in North America, Europe, Asia and in northern parts of Africa.

Like their larger cousin the Stoat, they have also been introduced to other countries (mainly as a form of pest control) like New Zealand and a number of other islands. However, they have had a detrimental effect on native wildlife. They are opportunistic predators and can be found in some urban areas especially near farms where there is an abundant, varied and tempting supply of food.

DIET

The weasel is a skilled and ferocious hunter, able to enter the burrows of its prey due to its small size and flexible spine They track small animals using tunnels that they make through the undergrowth and even under snow. Weasels are able to follow its prey back into its burrow and then catches it in its own home. Rodents such as mice and voles, along with lemmings further north, make up the bulk of the weasel's diet. They also occasionally eat birds.

They are also known to eat eggs and are able to kill animals larger than themselves like ducks and rabbits. Weasels must eat around a third of their body weight every day to survive, leading to them being such prolific hunters.

ENEMIES

Despite their fast and dexterous nature, their small size means that they are preyed upon by a number of predators throughout their home range. Birds of Prey such as owls, hawks and eagles that are able to spot them from high in the sky are the most common predators, along with foxes and snakes. They are also preyed upon by domestic cats and dogs in areas where they live close to people.

SUITABILITY AS PETS

Don't let the cute faces of weasels influence your opinion about their demeanor; they are known to be vicious creatures! They don't normally attack humans, unless provoked, but they will attack your other house pets. They are small and could easily be stepped on. prompting them to strike out by biting.

Keeping a wild weasel as a pet is something you might want to reconsider if you have other pets. The cousin of the weasel, a ferret, is a good pet and easy to tame. Some people have been able to keep a weasel as a pet, but this may not be a very good choice for you.

In some areas, it is illegal to keep a wild weasel as a pet, so be sure to check the laws in your area if you are thinking about a pet weasel.

COLOR ME

COLOR ME

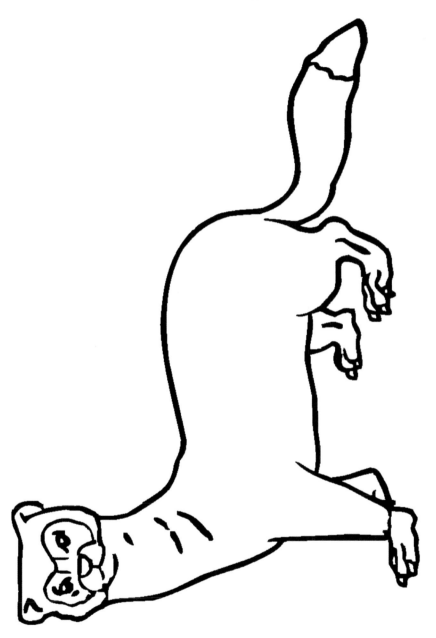

COLOR ME

COLOR ME

COLOR ME

COLOR ME

COLOR ME

COLOR ME

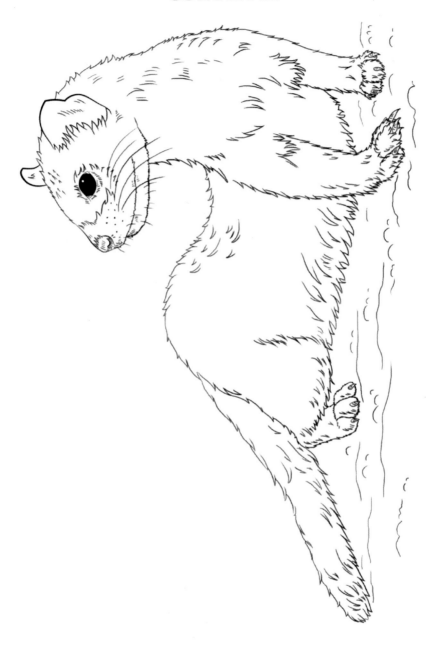

Please leave me a review here:

LisaStrattin.com/Review-Vol-235

For more Kindle Downloads Visit Lisa Strattin Author Page on Amazon Author Central

amazon.com/author/lisastrattin

To see upcoming titles, visit my website at LisaStrattin.com– most books available on Kindle!

LisaStrattin.com

FREE BOOK

FOR ALL SUBSCRIBERS – SIGN UP NOW

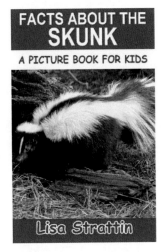

LisaStrattin.com/Subscribe-Here

LisaStrattin.com/Facebook

LisaStrattin.com/Youtube